Life BRIGHTENERS for Kids

H. Curtis & Karen McDaniel

WATERBROOK
PRESS

LIFE BRIGHTENERS FOR KIDS
PUBLISHED BY WATERBROOK PRESS
2375 Telstar Drive, Suite 160
Colorado Springs, Colorado 80920
A division of Random House, Inc.

All Scripture quotations, unless otherwise indicated, are taken from *The Message*. Copyright © 1993, 1994, 1995, 1996, 2000, 2001, 2002. Used by permission of NavPress Publishing Group. Scripture quotations marked (NIV) are taken from the *Holy Bible, New International Version*®. NIV®. Copyright © 1973, 1978, 1984 by International Bible Society. Used by permission of Zondervan Publishing House. All rights reserved.

ISBN 1-57856-723-8

Copyright © 2004 by H. Curtis McDaniel and Karen McDaniel

All rights reserved. No part of this book may be reproduced or transmitted in any form or by any means, electronic or mechanical, including photocopying and recording, or by any information storage and retrieval system, without permission in writing from the publisher.

WATERBROOK and its deer design logo are registered trademarks of WaterBrook Press, a division of Random House, Inc.

Printed in Canada
2004—First Edition

10 9 8 7 6 5 4 3 2 1

Since this work is an attempt to equip parents to encourage their grade-school children, we want to dedicate this in loving gratitude to our parents—the late Henry Curtis McDaniel Sr., Velma R. "Babs" McDaniel, the late Abraham David Preston, and Joan W. Preston—for providing us with a godly upbringing and loving parental influence that has been passed on from us to our children, Curtis McDaniel III, Megan McDaniel, and Heather McDaniel. May God, our great Savior, receive the glory, and may homes be strengthened in the fear and nurture of the Lord Jesus.

ACKNOWLEDGMENTS

Special thanks go to the following:

To our special friends John Stitt, MD, his wife, Dina, and their children, John Michael, Mary Elizabeth, and James Hunter, for their help in the project, especially Mary Elizabeth, who gave us good insight and help by reading the entire manuscript.

To our many family members, friends, and faithful prayer partners in Virginia; the St. Louis area; Montgomery, Alabama; Middle Tennessee; southern Kentucky; Fort Lauderdale, Florida; and Butler, Pennsylvania, for their faithful intercession for this work. Thank you for your help, encouragement, and prayers for us.

Introduction

Touch Your Child's Heart While You're Apart

The world is a daily battleground for the souls of our children. When our sons and daughters are away from us—with friends, at school, or practicing sports—they often find themselves in an environment that is hostile to the values we uphold as Christian families.

How can parents encourage their children when they need it the most—when the pressures of peers and the power of ungodly influences seek to lead them astray? Many children want to live for Christ. However, some are mocked by other students when they carry their Bibles at school. How can we encourage our kids to keep their eyes fixed upon Jesus all day long? How can we help provide an added injection of Christian truth to help them get through a tough day?

Life Brighteners for Kids is designed to equip parents to encourage their elementary-school- and middle-school-age children to take the Word of God with them. The ninety messages of encouragement enable parents to bring the truths and themes of Scripture to light in their children's hearts and souls. Each day's word of encouragement includes a timely scripture along with a related "life brightener" thought—specific guidance to encourage and strengthen our children's lives.

How to Use Life Brighteners

The entries in this book are organized under thirty practical topics, with three pertinent messages under each topic. The back of each page gives you an opportunity to write a personal note to your child. Then simply fold the page and insert it into your child's backpack or lunch bag. Sending your child off with a personal Life Brightener will take only seconds, but the impact will last all day long!

Some of the messages are more appropriate for older children, while others are written more simply to speak to younger kids. You can choose the words of encouragement and wisdom that fit your child's particular challenges and needs. Each day's Life Brightener enables you to do the following:

- Give your child a biblical pick-me-up for the day.
- Communicate your care while you and your child are apart.
- Lead your child to see the beauty and adventure of a personal relationship with Jesus Christ.
- Motivate your growing child to apply the truths of Scripture by offering practical suggestions.
- Equip your child to be an effective witness to others.

As you send your child off with these Life Brighteners, ask the Holy Spirit to use the Word of God to encourage, to shape, and to impact his or her life for Christ.

Acceptance

God Helps Us

...God is there, ready to help....
HEBREWS 13:6

Today's Life Brightener

Sometimes it's hard to get along with a teacher, a coach, or another kid at school. It's a good thing God promises to help us. Remember to ask God for his help today. He'll give it!

Special Notes:

Acceptance

God's Love

So reach out and welcome one another to God's glory.
Jesus did it; now you do it!
ROMANS 15:7

Today's Life Brightener

Some people really get on your nerves. When someone bugs you, think about how much God loves that person.

Special Notes:

Acceptance

Showing Love

...do this with humility and discipline—not in fits and starts, but steadily, pouring yourselves out for each other in acts of love.
EPHESIANS 4:2

Today's Life Brightener

Jesus accepts you in spite of your mistakes. Can you think of someone *you* need to accept?

Special Notes:

The Bible

Happiness

...you thrill to GOD's Word....
Psalm 1:2

Today's Life Brightener

What makes you happier than anything else? Do you enjoy reading the Bible? When you get home today, let's read it together!

Special Notes:

THE BIBLE

Think About It

...you chew on Scripture day and night.
PSALM 1:2

Today's Life Brightener

Cows chew and swallow, then regurgitate their food and chew it some more. In a sense, that's what God wants us to do with his Word. So go ahead—chew!

Special Notes:

THE BIBLE

Growing Stronger

You're a tree replanted in Eden, bearing fresh fruit every month,
never dropping a leaf, always in blossom.

PSALM 1:3

Today's Life Brightener

The more you run, the stronger your legs get. The more you regularly read the Bible, the more you grow!

Special Notes:

Choices

A Better Solution

...don't try to figure out everything on your own.
Proverbs 3:5

Today's Life Brightener

You know how sometimes a math problem just seems too hard to solve? Life can be like that at times. But God's wisdom can help you. Ask for it today!

Special Notes:

CHOICES

The Right Choice

...As for me and my family, we'll worship God.

JOSHUA 24:15

Today's Life Brightener

Every day we can choose to love and obey God or to do our own thing. What is your choice today?

Special Notes:

CHOICES

Good Thoughts

...No one makes a fool of God. What a person plants,
he will harvest.

GALATIANS 6:7

Today's Life Brightener

Life is like planting a garden: whatever you put in your mind, it will grow there. Are you reading and watching things that help you love and think about God?

Special Notes:

●---●

●---●

●---●

●---●

DOING WHAT'S RIGHT

Count on Jesus

But the Master never lets us down.
He'll stick by you and protect you....
2 Thessalonians 3:3

Today's Life Brightener

Jesus never forgets what you need. You can count on him to help and protect you!

Special Notes:

DOING WHAT'S RIGHT

Doing Your Best

...My heart took delight in all my work,
and this was the reward for all my labor.
ECCLESIASTES 2:10 (NIV)

Today's Life Brightener

You've worked hard and done great in school this year. I'm proud of you!

Special Notes:

DOING WHAT'S RIGHT

A Good Example

Let every detail in your lives—words, actions, whatever—be done in the name of the Master, Jesus....

COLOSSIANS 3:17

Today's Life Brightener

Whether you're in school, playing a game, or spending time with a friend, remember this: your words and actions can help other kids see the love of Jesus.

Special Notes:

EFFORT

Hard Work

Hard work always pays off....
PROVERBS 14:23

Today's Life Brightener

There's no substitute for hard work at school and around the house. God says it pays off!

Special Notes:

EFFORT

God's Help

...only crazy people would think they could complete
by their own efforts what was begun by God....
GALATIANS 3:3

Today's Life Brightener

No matter how hard you try, you still need God's help. Let him guide you today!

Special Notes:

●------------------------------------●

●------------------------------------●

●------------------------------------●

●------------------------------------●

EFFORT

Getting Tired?

So let's not allow ourselves to get fatigued doing good....
GALATIANS 6:9

Today's Life Brightener

Schoolwork makes you tired. But just think how good you'll feel at the end of the year. God sees your effort and promises to help!

Special Notes:

ETERNAL LIFE

God Saves Us!

...we've been given a brand-new life and have everything to live for, including a future in heaven....
1 Peter 1:3-4

Today's Life Brightener

God didn't have to save you, but he did. Thank God for loving you so much!

Special Notes:

ETERNAL LIFE

The Cross

...to us who are being saved [the message of the cross]
is the power of God.
1 CORINTHIANS 1:18 (NIV)

Today's Life Brightener

The cross didn't start out as jewelry to wear on a necklace. Jesus died on a cross for our sins. What do you think of when you see a cross?

Special Notes:

ETERNAL LIFE

Do What's Right

...Jesus Christ rescued us from this evil world we're in
by offering himself as a sacrifice for our sins....
GALATIANS 1:3-4

Today's Life Brightener

It's hard to do the right thing when other kids make fun of you. But Jesus helps us do what's right even when it's not easy. He's pleased with you, and so am I!

Special Notes:

FEAR

God's Power

For God did not give us a spirit of timidity,
but a spirit of power....
2 Timothy 1:7 (NIV)

Today's Life Brightener

God is big enough to help you get over your fears. He promises to help you!

Special Notes:

FEAR

God's Protection

> I will lie down and sleep in peace,
> for you alone, O LORD,
> make me dwell in safety.
>
> PSALM 4:8 (NIV)

Today's Life Brightener

Do you ever feel scared at night? God always watches over you. Just ask him, and he'll keep you safe.

Special Notes:

FEAR

God's Spirit

We have not received the spirit of the world
but the Spirit who is from God....
1 CORINTHIANS 2:12 (NIV)

Today's Life Brightener

Jesus lives inside us through his Holy Spirit. I love seeing him at work in your life, helping you!

Special Notes:

Following Jesus

Think First

Watch your words and hold your tongue;
you'll save yourself a lot of grief.

Proverbs 21:23

Today's Life Brightener

You can avoid big problems by thinking before you open your mouth. Ask God to help you think before you speak.

Special Notes:

Following Jesus

Acting Like Jesus

...Christ lives in me. The life you see me living is not "mine," but it is lived by faith in the Son of God....

GALATIANS 2:20

Today's Life Brightener

Your actions can give people an idea of how Jesus wants us to live. So today, live for Jesus!

Special Notes:

Following Jesus

Gentleness

But the fruit of the Spirit is...gentleness....
GALATIANS 5:22-23 (NIV)

Today's Life Brightener

God wants us to be kind and gentle and to treat people with respect. How can you do that today?

Special Notes:

FORGIVENESS

God's Forgiveness

...the blood of Jesus, his Son, purifies us from all sin.
1 John 1:7 (NIV)

Today's Life Brightener

Have you ever felt guilty? God forgives us when we admit our sins. Just tell him now!

Special Notes:

FORGIVENESS

Real Freedom

...you are not a slave, but a child [of God]....

GALATIANS 4:7

Today's Life Brightener

Slaves have no hope or future unless their owners decide to set them free. That's like what God did for you! You have been set free from sin's power.

Special Notes:

FORGIVENESS

God's Promise

...if we admit our sins...he won't let us down;
he'll be true to himself. He'll forgive our sins....

1 JOHN 1:9

Today's Life Brightener

The Lord promises to give us complete forgiveness, and he always does what he promises. That's how much he loves you!

Special Notes:

FORGIVING OTHERS

Hurt Feelings

Be gentle with one another, sensitive. Forgive one another....

EPHESIANS 4:32

Today's Life Brightener

When someone hurts your feelings, it's hard to forgive that person. But God says we need to. Ask him to help you forgive others.

Special Notes:

FORGIVING OTHERS

Keep It Up!

Blessed are the merciful,
for they will be shown mercy.
MATTHEW 5:7 (NIV)

Today's Life Brightener

Showing mercy means forgiving other people and loving those who are hurting. I have seen your kindness toward others. Keep it up!

Special Notes:

Forgiving Others

Forgiving Is Hard

Keep us forgiven with you and forgiving others.
Keep us safe from ourselves and the Devil....
Matthew 6:12-13

Today's Life Brightener

If you want God's forgiveness, you need to forgive people who hurt you. Ask God to help you do something really hard: to forgive that kid who keeps annoying you.

Special Notes:

FRIENDSHIP

Keeping a Promise

A gossip betrays a confidence,
but a trustworthy man keeps a secret.
PROVERBS 11:13 (NIV)

Today's Life Brightener

Has a friend told you something personal? Remember, God gave us two ears and one mouth. It's better to listen than to speak!

Special Notes:

FRIENDSHIP

A Great Friend

A friend loves at all times....
PROVERBS 17:17 (NIV)

Today's Life Brightener

Friends are loyal to one another in good times *and* bad times. Will you be that kind of friend today?

Special Notes:

FRIENDSHIP

The Best Friends

Wounds from a friend can be trusted....
PROVERBS 27:6 (NIV)

Today's Life Brightener

A good friend will tell you when you're messing up. It might make you mad. But remember that real friends want what is best for you. God loves that type of friend!

Special Notes:

GENEROSITY

Giving to God

Honor GOD with everything you own;
give him the first and the best.
PROVERBS 3:9

Today's Life Brightener

You don't have much money, but God does good things for you when you give part of your money back to him. Let's think of a way to do that!

Special Notes:

GENEROSITY

A Free Blessing

The world of the generous gets larger and larger;
the world of the stingy gets smaller and smaller.
PROVERBS 11:24

Today's Life Brightener

When you give to God, he returns a blessing. Whatever you give to God pleases him!

Special Notes:

GENEROSITY

Wanting to Give

...the righteous give without sparing.
PROVERBS 21:26 (NIV)

Today's Life Brightener

When you love the Lord, you want to give him something. What runs through your mind when the offering plate is passed at church?

Special Notes:

God's Love

A Gift from God

This is the kind of love we are talking about—
not that we once upon a time loved God, but that he loved us
and sent his Son as a sacrifice to clear away our sins....

1 John 4:10

Today's Life Brightener

It's fun to get gifts. But it's even better to give a present to someone you love. That's how God loves us. He gave us his Son!

Special Notes:

GOD'S LOVE

The Greatest Love

...First we were loved, now we love. He loved us first.
1 JOHN 4:19

Today's Life Brightener

God doesn't love you only when you're good. He loves you all the time. And so do I!

Special Notes:

GOD'S LOVE

God Protects You

He's a...personal bodyguard to the candid and sincere.
PROVERBS 2:7

Today's Life Brightener

God promises to protect us when we're honest and sincere. Today he is protecting you!

Special Notes:

GOD'S PROMISES

God Says You're Great!

...With God on our side like this, how can we lose?

ROMANS 8:31

Today's Life Brightener

If God were a team captain in gym class, he'd choose you! Nothing is too big for you and God to do together.

Special Notes:

●------------------------------------●

●------------------------------------●

●------------------------------------●

●------------------------------------●

God's Promises

God Keeps Promises

Let's keep a firm grip on the promises that keep us going.
He always keeps his word.
HEBREWS 10:23

Today's Life Brightener

When God makes a promise to love you, he keeps it. Look for his love today!

Special Notes:

God's Promises

God's Protection

But the Master never lets us down.
He'll stick by you and protect you from evil.
2 Thessalonians 3:3

Today's Life Brightener

Jesus promised to protect you from temptation. When things get hard, tell him you need his protection!

Special Notes:

God's Strength

Real Power

I can do everything through him who gives me strength.
PHILIPPIANS 4:13 (NIV)

Today's Life Brightener

Whatever you need to do today, Jesus has the strength to help you. Let your friends see God's power shine through you!

Special Notes:

God's Strength

Tired Today?

For even young people tire and drop out....
But those who wait upon GOD get fresh strength....
ISAIAH 40:30–31

Today's Life Brightener

When you want to give up, God gives you strength. When you're worn out, he's there to help. I'm here to help too!

Special Notes:

GOD'S STRENGTH

Safety

GOD's name is a place of protection—
good people can run there and be safe.

PROVERBS 18:10

Today's Life Brightener

When we're close to God, we're safe. I'm glad God is watching out for you!

Special Notes:

Good Attitudes

Showing Kindness

...Put yourself aside, and help others get ahead.
PHILIPPIANS 2:3

Today's Life Brightener

God wants us to focus on other people, not just ourselves. Who can you be kind to today?

Special Notes:

GOOD ATTITUDES

Feeling Mad?

...make sure it's all gone for good: bad temper, irritability, meanness....

COLOSSIANS 3:8

Today's Life Brightener

God wants us to clean up our bad attitudes and bad language. So when you get mad, ask God to change your attitude.

Special Notes:

Good Attitudes

Tell the Truth

Truth lasts;
lies are here today, gone tomorrow.
PROVERBS 12:19

Today's Life Brightener

God is pleased when you tell the whole truth. Ask him to help you be honest today!

Special Notes:

GRATITUDE

You're a Gift

O my soul, bless GOD, don't forget a single blessing!
PSALM 103:2

Today's Life Brightener

God loves to give us good things. And on my list of good things, you're at the top!

Special Notes:

GRATITUDE

God Is Good

...Thank GOD! And why? Because he's good, because his love lasts.
PSALM 106:1

Today's Life Brightener

Why do we need to thank God? It's because he is always good. Thank him today for all the good things he does for you.

Special Notes:

GRATITUDE

Tell God "Thanks"

...thanking God the Father every step of the way.

COLOSSIANS 3:17

Today's Life Brightener

You can thank God while hanging out with friends and even when you're taking a test. Stop for a minute and thank God for something right now.

Special Notes:

JOY

God's Joy

But the fruit of the Spirit is...joy....
GALATIANS 5:22 (NIV)

Today's Life Brightener

You feel happy when you get a good grade or when your friends are nice to you. God's joy is different: it comes when we obey Jesus!

Special Notes:

JOY

God Brings Joy

...The nights of crying your eyes out
give way to days of laughter.
PSALM 30:5

Today's Life Brightener

If you're sad about something, remember that sadness doesn't last forever. God will bring back your joy!

Special Notes:

JOY

Rejoice in God

But may all who seek you
rejoice and be glad in you....
PSALM 40:16 (NIV)

Today's Life Brightener

The best way to be glad is to seek God with everything you've got. He's waiting to give you his joy!

Special Notes:

KINDNESS

Being Kind

...always try to be kind to each other....
1 Thessalonians 5:15 (NIV)

Today's Life Brightener

It's not easy to be kind to everyone at school or at home. But find just one person to be kind to today. Go on—give it a try!

Special Notes:

KINDNESS

Loving Others

...The only thing that counts is faith expressing itself
through love.
GALATIANS 5:6 (NIV)

Today's Life Brightener

When you love people who are mean or unfair, you're showing Jesus that you love him. I've seen you love others like that!

Special Notes:

KINDNESS

Who Needs Help?

...let us do good to all people....
GALATIANS 6:10 (NIV)

Today's Life Brightener

Think of a way to help someone, even if it's a small thing. Small things make a big difference!

Special Notes:

LOVING GOD

Obeying God

Love means following his commandments....
2 JOHN 6

Today's Life Brightener

Obeying God is the best way to show him that you love him. It means a lot when others see you do the right thing!

Special Notes:

LOVING GOD

God Is Working

..."My Father is always at his work...."
JOHN 5:17 (NIV)

Today's Life Brightener

God is always working in people's lives. I see him working more and more in your life too. What do you see God doing?

Special Notes:

LOVING GOD

God's Strength

...those who hunger and thirst for righteousness...will be filled.
MATTHEW 5:6 (NIV)

Today's Life Brightener

Even when you try really hard, you can't be good *all* the time. That's why you need God's help. When you call him, he will hear!

Special Notes:

OBEDIENCE

The Brightest Light

But if we walk in the light, God himself being the light...
1 JOHN 1:7

Today's Life Brightener

Have you ever walked through a dark room and stubbed your toe? We need light to show us the way. When you obey Jesus, you have God's light!

Special Notes:

OBEDIENCE

God Is Nearby

For the LORD watches over the way of the righteous....
PSALM 1:6 (NIV)

Today's Life Brightener

God takes care of those who obey him. Remember, he is always with you because he wants the best for you!

Special Notes:

OBEDIENCE

God's Spirit

Since we live by the Spirit, let us keep in step with the Spirit.
GALATIANS 5:25 (NIV)

Today's Life Brightener

The Holy Spirit lives inside you. He will guide you and help you every step of the way.

Special Notes:

PARENTS AND FAMILY

Great Advice

Take good counsel and accept correction—
that's the way to live wisely and well.

PROVERBS 19:20

Today's Life Brightener

Sometimes adults really bug you. They're always telling you to do things. But adults can give you great advice. So listen up!

Special Notes:

PARENTS AND FAMILY

Love at Home

...Love others as you love yourself....
GALATIANS 5:14

Today's Life Brightener

The Bible tells us to love God first, then to love other people as much as we love ourselves. When you come home today, make sure you tell someone "I love you!"

Special Notes:

Parents and Family

Tough Love

It's the child he loves that GOD corrects;
a father's delight is behind all this.

PROVERBS 3:12

Today's Life Brightener

Sometimes God uses moms and dads to correct their children's bad behavior. It's meant for your good in love. Honest!

Special Notes:

PRAYER

God Always Listens

Pray all the time.

1 Thessalonians 5:17

Today's Life Brightener

God wants you to talk to him all day long. He's interested in everything, so tell him what's on your mind!

Special Notes:

PRAYER

God Cares

...GOD doesn't miss a move you make;
he's aware of every step you take.
PROVERBS 5:21

Today's Life Brightener

God knows what's happening to you. When you feel lonely or sad, remember that God cares. And so do I!

Special Notes:

PRAYER

God Hears Us

To the LORD I cry aloud, and he answers me....
PSALM 3:4 (NIV)

Today's Life Brightener

Sometimes God waits before he helps us. He's waiting for us to ask! Go ahead—ask for some help.

Special Notes:

RESPECT

Following God

You're blessed when you're at the end of your rope.
With less of you there is more of God and his rule.

MATTHEW 5:3

Today's Life Brightener

Moses was a great leader, but he knew his limitations. He was humble enough to follow God's instructions. I know you're strong enough to follow God!

Special Notes:

RESPECT

Respect Everyone

Show proper respect to everyone....
1 PETER 2:17 (NIV)

Today's Life Brightener

Showing respect means you consider other people to be valuable. Since God values everyone, we are to respect everyone we meet!

Special Notes:

RESPECT

Pray for Leaders

Appreciate your pastoral leaders who gave you the Word of God....
HEBREWS 13:7

Today's Life Brightener

How often do you pray for your pastor and Sunday school teacher? Have you asked God to bless them this week? They have big jobs to do, so pray for them.

Special Notes:

●---------------------------------●

●---------------------------------●

●---------------------------------●

●---------------------------------●

SELF-CONTROL

The Strength to Resist

But the fruit of the Spirit is...self-control....
GALATIANS 5:22-23 (NIV)

Today's Life Brightener

Do you find yourself doing things you know you shouldn't? Ask God to give you self-control. He will help you!

Special Notes:

SELF-CONTROL

Guard Your Mind

God wants you to live a pure life....
1 Thessalonians 4:3

Today's Life Brightener

The things that are in your mind affect your actions and words. Please be careful what you read and watch!

Special Notes:

SELF-CONTROL

Watch Out!

Keep a firm grasp on both your character and your teaching....
1 Timothy 4:16

Today's Life Brightener

Be on the lookout for things that are bad for you. Let God's Word help you!

Special Notes:

TAKING SHORTCUTS

Don't Cheat

...you yourselves cheat and do wrong....
1 CORINTHIANS 6:8 (NIV)

Today's Life Brightener

It's tempting to take a dishonest shortcut. Keep in mind that God knows our thoughts and sees our actions.

Special Notes:

Taking Shortcuts

Taking a Test?

Keep your eyes straight ahead....
PROVERBS 4:25

Today's Life Brightener

Some kids try to get a better grade by looking at someone else's paper. But this doesn't please God. Who knows? Their answers could be wrong!

Special Notes:

Taking Shortcuts

Make Things Right

...Have I ever taken advantage of you...?
Bring your complaint and I'll make it right.
1 Samuel 12:3

Today's Life Brightener

Have you been unfair to someone? Talk to the person and try to make things right. You'll be glad you did!

Special Notes:

TRUST

Trust the Best

...I trust in God....
PSALM 56:11

Today's Life Brightener

It feels great to trust God, because he never disappoints us. He always wants what is best for you!

Special Notes:

TRUST

Trusting God

Trust GOD from the bottom of your heart....
PROVERBS 3:5

Today's Life Brightener

If you want God's help, you have to trust him. Trust means you will let him lead your life. Do you trust God that much?

Special Notes:

TRUST

God's Voice

Listen for GOD's voice in everything you do, everywhere you go;
he's the one who will keep you on track.

PROVERBS 3:6

Today's Life Brightener

Have you ever gotten lost? God keeps you on track so you can keep going in the right direction!

Special Notes:

TRUTH

A Pure Heart

Blessed are the pure in heart, for they will see God.
MATTHEW 5:8 (NIV)

Today's Life Brightener

The phrase "pure in heart" means being honest and truthful. If you live with a pure heart, Jesus says you will see God. That's awesome!

Special Notes:

TRUTH

Truthful Words

Honesty lives confident and carefree....
PROVERBS 10:9

Today's Life Brightener

When you're honest and tell the truth, you don't have to worry about what you said in the past. I'm glad you tell me the truth!

Special Notes:

TRUTH

God Loves the Truth

God can't stomach liars;
he loves the company of those who keep their word.
PROVERBS 12:22

Today's Life Brightener

You please God when you're consistent in telling the truth. Try it all day long and see what happens!

Special Notes:

WISDOM

Start with God

...the first step in learning is bowing down to GOD....
PROVERBS 1:7

Today's Life Brightener

If you want to do great things, start by getting to know God. Many of the greatest scientists, musicians, and leaders in history were Christians. I know you can do great things!

Special Notes:

WISDOM

God's Directions

...Lead me down the path of truth....
PSALM 25:5

Today's Life Brightener

In school, in sports, and when you're with friends and family, make sure God is number one in your life. When you do, he directs you!

Special Notes:

WISDOM

God Guides You

...GOD gives out Wisdom free....
PROVERBS 2:6

Today's Life Brightener

Is something bothering you at school, with your friends, or at home? Ask God for the wisdom to know what to do. He will guide you!

Special Notes:

WITNESSING

Make a Difference!

So don't be embarrassed to speak up for our Master....
2 TIMOTHY 1:8

Today's Life Brightener

Don't be afraid to tell your friends about Jesus. Use your words and actions to show God's love. You can make a difference!

Special Notes:

WITNESSING

Share God's Love

...you will be able to be my witnesses....
ACTS 1:8

Today's Life Brightener

Someone you talk to today needs to hear about Jesus's love. Look around. Ask God who needs his love.

Special Notes:

WITNESSING

Show God's Love

*...every time we get the chance,
let us work for the benefit of all....*
GALATIANS 6:10

Today's Life Brightener

Jesus wants us to work hard at helping others, just as he did. Think about your friends. Who needs to see God's love through you?

Special Notes: